MW00965050

Rice Boy

By SUNIL KURUVILLA

Christmas 2004

Rice Boy

Sunil Kuruvilla

*For Nicholas —
a great addition
to any playwright's library.
with love,
Lise*

Playwrights Canada Press
Toronto•Canada

Playwrights Canada Press
54 Wolseley St., 2nd floor Toronto, Ontario CANADA M5T 1A5
416-703-0013   fax 416-703-0059
orders@playwrightscanada.com • www.playwrightscanada.com

Playwrights Canada Press acknowledges the support of
the taxpayers of Canada and the province of Ontario through
The Canada Council for the Arts and the Ontario Arts Council.

Cover creative: Scott Thornley + Company Inc.
Production Editor: Jodi Armstrong

National Library of Canada Cataloguing in Publication

Kuruvilla, Sunil
    Rice boy / Sunil Kuruvilla.

A play.
ISBN 0-88754-672-2

    I. Title.

PS8571.U784R52 2003   C812'.54   C2003-900618-2
PR9199.3.K794R52 2003

First edition: March 2003.
Printed and bound by AGMV Marquis at Quebec, Canada.

For Mom and Dad

-to see everything and to realize the best and worst
of everything
is to love and not forget

from "To-"
by Al Purdy

INTRODUCTION

I start with a disclaimer: *Rice Boy* is not autobiographical. Unlike Tommy in the play, I have a mother and father, both loving and very much alive. That said, some of the folkloric and sensual elements in the play are rooted in the real. I met the bad luck tailor (escaping unscathed) and the fish seller on trips to India when I was a boy. Rosewater ice cream, sandalwood, and the drift of talcum in my grandfather's house inform the play as much as Oktoberfest, wiener schnitzel, and the smell of fried onions at the Harmony Lunch.

In South India, early each morning, women grind rice then use the resulting powder to create elaborate kolams or patterns on their front porch that disappear within hours. Originally, a Hindu cultural practice, now adopted by others, the creation and destruction of the kolam enacts the struggle to find pattern and stillness amidst the flux of life. A product of ache, *Rice Boy* is a collection of love stories that struggles with the transitory nature of home, memory, and affection. The characters in the play find it difficult to accept the kolam's message: all things are impermanent and should be celebrated for being so. But they try.

ACKNOWLEDGMENTS

P.K., Anna, and Deepa Kuruvilla.

Steph Adams, Mervin Antonio, Mark Bly, Martin Bragg, Jason Campbell, Lisa Channer, Micheline Chevrier, Rob Coelho, Lynn Cohen, John Dias, John Glore, Anna Gupta, Mandy Hackett, Amy Handelsman, Amir Haque, Len Jenkin, Joyce Ketay, Jennifer Kiger, John Kuruvilla and family, Alistair MacLeod, Gillian Lynne-Davies, Donald Margulies, Anthony Minghella, Chiori Miyagawa, Eric Overmyer, Robin Pitcher, Sharon Pollock, Jean Randich, Martha Reeves, Lisa Rodrigues, Edwin Sanchez, Kim Selody, Far Shariat, Beverly Simons, Wendy Streeter, Rebecca Taichman, Pier Carlo Talenti, Eappen Thomas and family, Chuck Thompson, David Thompson, John Turci-Escobar, Iris Turcott, Joe Varkey, Mac Wellman, The Williams family, Stan Wojewodski, The Canada Council for the Arts, Ontario Arts Council.

Special thanks to Liz Diamond and Chay Yew who directed productions of *Rice Boy* – their kindness is as big as their talent.

Rice Boy had its world premiere at the Yale Repertory Theatre, New Haven, Connecticut, in October 2000, with the following company:

Tommy	Wayne Kesserman
Tina	Angel Desai
Father	Sean T. Krishnan
Uncle	Sanjiv Jhaveri
Auntie	Shaheen Vaaz
Granny	Yolande Bavan
Servant girl	Anita Gandhi
Fish Seller/Clerk/	
Umbrella Man/Nut Seller	Ajay Naidu
Mr. Harris/Mennonite Farmer	Colin Lane

Directed by Liz Diamond
Scenic Design by Tobin Ross Ost
Costume Design by Cameron Lee Roberts
Lighting Design by Matthew Richards
Sound Design by David Budries
Fight Director: Rick Sordelet
Stage Management by Rachana V. Singh
Dramaturgy by Claudia Wilsch
Casting by Johnson-Liff Associates, Ltd.

———•—•———

Rice Boy's west-coast premiere was at the Mark Taper Forum, Los Angeles, California, April 2001, directed by Chay Yew
.

———•—•———

Rice Boy had its Canadian premiere at the Canadian Stage Company, Toronto, Ontario, March 2003, directed by Micheline Chevrier.

CHARACTERS

Tommy	Boy, 12.
Tina	Tommy's cousin, can't walk, rolls on a cart, 16
Father	Tommy's father, 35
Uncle	Tina's father, 40
Auntie	Tina's mother, 35
Granny	Mother of Father and Uncle
Servant girl	Ex-wife of Fish Seller, 25

Fish Seller
Clerk
Umbrella Man
Nut Seller

Mr. Harris	German man, 40
Mennonite Farmer	

One actor can play Fish Seller, Clerk, Umbrella Man, and Nut Seller.
One actor can play Mr. Harris and Mennonite Farmer.

SETTING

This play is set in Canada and India in 1975.

Scene: India
—•—•—

Summer 1975. In Kottayam, a town in south India, on the front porch of UNCLE's house, TINA kneels on the floor trying to design an elaborate pattern made from rice powder and water.

TINA   Water into your palm. Water onto the floor. Finger into rice powder. Powder onto the water.

GRANNY enters carrying two cups of coffee. She watches TINA slide on the floor.

Scene: Canada
—•—•—

Six months later: Winter 1975. In Kitchener, a city in Canada, TOMMY sits in a tree as his FATHER, in a dhoti, sleeps on the kitchen counter, covered by a cotton sheet. The boy watches GRANNY and TINA design the rice pattern, remembering.

FATHER   I'm awake sir. Come down from the tree.

No reaction.

Come in the house boss!

No reaction.

What's wrong with you? Six months we've been back in Canada and you still just sit dead in the branches. Leave the tree alone. Come take care of your father.

No reaction.

Tommy! Do you hear what I'm meaning?

No reaction.

In India, children listen to their parents. *(beat)* Idiot – say something!

TOMMY   Did you go to work today?

> *No reaction.*

Did you go to work today?

> *No reaction.*

You said you were going to.

> *No reaction.*

All you do is sleep.

> *No reaction.*

All you do is sleep.

FATHER   I'm tired. It's the time change.

TOMMY   We came back from India six months ago! *(beat)*
You're going to lose your job again.

FATHER   Show respect! Is this the way a son talks to the father!
I'll spank the skin off your hand.

TOMMY   Why are you just sleeping on the kitchen counter?

FATHER   I'm sad! Come down from the tree and rub my head.

> *TOMMY climbs down to the lower branches of the tree
> then steps through the window into the kitchen. The boy
> starts to massage his FATHER's head.*

Ten years it took us to go back to India. I was so
excited but then we get there. All I did was think
about your mother. I was so alone.

> *FATHER takes TOMMY's hand and smells.*

Your mother's hand. It smelled like this skin. The gold
sari she'd wear to church. Bright as a flag. We'd come
home and I'd unwrap her. Going in circles, moving
away from her body and then in the end, moving

close. Rolling on the ground. Silk in the mouth. The taste like hair. When you get older you stop thinking. All you do is remember. I'm going to stand up.

FATHER gets down from the counter and stands.

Maybe next summer we go back to India again. Maybe next time things go better.

TOMMY   No! Next summer, we should do camping. We can go to Algonquin Park. Or do African Lion Safari. Do what normal people do. Mini-golf. Water-ski.

FATHER   Those are Canadian things.

TOMMY   That's okay.

FATHER   I can't do those things.

TOMMY   Try.

FATHER lies back on the counter.

FATHER   I was a math professor once.

TOMMY   I like when you worked at Kitchener Datsun.

FATHER   Now the Mother's Pizza. The cheese smell when I come home and take shower. Che! I burn so much incense.

TOMMY   I like when you bring garlic bread home.

FATHER   You're just like me, don't forget. Doesn't matter if you were born in Canada. You're still Indian Tommy. Be proud of who you are.

TOMMY   Your next job, you should work at Rockway Fish and Chips.

FATHER   You can be Canadian when you go to school but not in this house. Cut a banana, pour some oil.

> *TOMMY takes a milk carton from the fridge and
> starts to read the side panel.*

I'll go to the farmer's market tomorrow and buy
you a goat. A big, healthy one. We can kill it in the
basement. No stink. We'll open the windows and use
the fan. You can make me a nice curry.

TOMMY   The boy on the milk carton. He's from St. Jacobs.

FATHER   Did you wash my socks?

TOMMY   Yes.

FATHER   And my benyan?

TOMMY   Yeah.

FATHER   I hope you ironed my shirts. I don't like when it's
rough.

> *Silence.*

Keep me awake boy. Give the story about India. One
about our trip. Give a happy ending this time.

> *TOMMY continues staring at the milk carton.*

You used to rub my head and make banana chips.
Now you can't even give one story when I ask. You
just sit like a stick in the tree. In India, I could thrash
you so hard but here – I'd get arrested.

> *TOMMY continues staring at the milk carton.*

Wife, are you watching all this? How did this happen
to me?

> *TOMMY exits, taking his milk carton with him.
> FATHER remains on the counter.*

I think about you now more than any other part of
the day. I see so much in the dark.

Beat.

The brain remembers more at night.

Scene: India
—•—•—

GRANNY continues to watch TINA design.

GRANNY   Water into your palm. Water onto the floor. Finger into rice powder. Powder onto the water. Good Tina. You will do this every morning like the other wives in this village.

TINA   Mother doesn't do this.

GRANNY   You will wake before your husband and get water. You will grind rice into powder and make a pattern, moving away from the door. When your husband wakes he will walk through your design, the powder that touched your fingers, sticking to his feet. In a few hours the pattern is gone. In the evening, your husband returns to a blank porch. In the dark, you start again, this time moving toward the door, toward the bed where your husband waits. As he sleeps, the night lifts your design. The fan above your head swirls a cloud of powder as your husband dreams dreams as sweet as sandalwood. He wakes up to find you staring into his face. His hands tie up in your hair.

TINA   My fingers don't work. I'll never get a husband.

GRANNY gives the coffee cups to TINA and starts to design.

GRANNY   Don't worry. We will practice like this every morning before you get married. Like this. Make a design. Tell a story. Where's your Grandfather?

TINA   He died a few months back. You always forget. At night you try to find him. The Servant Girl has to lie in the doorway of your bedroom. You don't see her and you step on her. She wakes up and tells you Grandpa is dead.

GRANNY	Drink the coffee then.

> *TOMMY runs from the house, through the design, his AUNTIE twisting his ear.*

TOMMY	No Auntie!
AUNTIE	You come back inside and go pop!
TOMMY	I'm not sitting on that toilet.
AUNTIE	You haven't had a bowel movement in 10 days!
TOMMY	I'll go when I get back to Canada. The toilets are clean there.
AUNTIE	Do pop!
TOMMY	Not that toilet!
AUNTIE	You don't have to sit.
TOMMY	I want toilet paper.
AUNTIE	Use your hand – learn to use water. You're going to pop open!
TOMMY	Let go of my ear – you're paining me!

> *TOMMY breaks free and scales a coconut tree.*

AUNTIE	Come down.
TOMMY	India. All I do is sit under the fan and read *Reader's Digest*.
AUNTIE	Come down.
TOMMY	I hate this place. I want a hot dog!
AUNTIE	Enough Tommy!
TOMMY	You're not my mother.

AUNTIE   Yes I am. Every woman in this village is your mother. You respect them and you listen. Where's your father? He's always leaving.

TOMMY   *(points from above)* He's throwing rocks at the river again.

AUNTIE   Where's your father?

TINA   I don't know mother.

TOMMY   I don't see him.

AUNTIE   We're going to push your stomach until you explode. *(to GRANNY)* Watch him. Make sure he doesn't fall. Only monkeys climb coconut trees.

> *AUNTIE exits.*

TOMMY   The Servant Girl made your egg.

GRANNY   And Bombay Toast?

TOMMY   Yes. Bombay Toast.

GRANNY   Don't fall.

> *GRANNY exits into the house.*

TOMMY   Who are you?

TINA   Your cousin.

TOMMY   Your legs are weird.

TINA   They don't work.

TOMMY   I can see everything from up here.

TINA   What do you see?

TOMMY   The Fish Man is riding his bicycle. Some men are pushing a taxi. A boy is running beside a tire, slapping it with a stick.

TINA	What does the river look like?
TOMMY	I don't know. Water.
TINA	No – Look.
TOMMY	It's dirty.
TINA	Keep talking.
TOMMY	Your mother is running to the river. I could slip.
TINA	Go higher.
TOMMY	I've never climbed a tree before. They aren't this big in Canada.

TOMMY keeps climbing.

TINA	Are people swimming?
TOMMY	Some.
TINA	How many? Count.
TOMMY	Four. Four men.
TINA	How far is it from here?
TOMMY	My father is sitting down and covering his face. I think he's crying.
TINA	What else do you see?
TOMMY	I'm tired.
TINA	No. Describe. Keep going. What do the houses look like? Are they different from this one? You can be my eyes. How wide is the road? What do the buses look like? And the trucks? They paint big names on the front, don't they? I've heard them drive by all my life.
TOMMY	You've never seen a truck!

TINA	I've never left this house.
TOMMY	Stupid Girl!
TINA	Read the trucks. Tell me what you see.

TOMMY starts to read the names on the trucks:

TOMMY	Vymol. Raju. Georgie. Simon. Saju. Lisa. I always look for "Tommy" but I haven't found one yet.
TINA	Find "Tina."
TOMMY	There's no "Tina." The trucks have boy's names.
TINA	You found "Lisa."
TOMMY	I'll find "Tommy" before I find "Tina." First one wins.
TINA	You could lie. I wouldn't know.
TOMMY	You could trust me.
TINA	That hammering sound. Are the women cutting into trees?
TOMMY	Yes. What are they doing? They're hammering nails and putting up coconut shells.
TINA	They're collecting rubber. It comes from the tree.
TOMMY	Like maple syrup.
TINA	You saw that the last time you were here. You must have. All I see are the rubber trees.
TOMMY	I don't remember the last trip.
TINA	Your mother died. You don't remember that?
TOMMY	I was too little.
TINA	Stupid Boy.

TOMMY	I can see the whole world. What can you see?
TINA	Stop talking.
TOMMY	I see the sari store. The water fountain. The post office.
TINA	Stop it.
TOMMY	I see chickens running through the church. I see the powder factory and the butcher shop. What can you see?
TINA	The bottom of your feet.
TOMMY	Can you see the powder factory? Smart Girl, what can you see?
TINA	Blood.
TOMMY	Where?
TINA	On the ground. You're dripping.
TOMMY	My nose is bleeding. Get me a Kleenex!
TINA	Get it yourself.

> *TINA sits on her cart and rolls herself into the house.*

TOMMY	Slide close. I want to drip on your head.
	Ugly turtle. Slide away. Straighten your skirt. You almost showed me your legs. I don't want to get sick.

> *TOMMY remains in the tree, moving in the branches, trying to drip his blood in different directions. SERVANT GIRL enters with GRANNY brushing the old woman's false teeth.*

GRANNY	Good, you didn't fall. Where's Tina?
TOMMY	In the house.

GRANNY   I heard you talking. Good boy Tommy. She's usually so shy.

> *GRANNY takes her false teeth from the SERVANT GIRL. The FISHSELLER enters, walking his bicycle. He opens his basket.*

**FISH
SELLER**   Kingfish Auntie?

GRANNY   What else?

**FISH
SELLER**   Take some trout.

GRANNY   No.

**FISH
SELLER**   Trout Auntie,

GRANNY   What else?

**FISH
SELLER**   I don't catch the fish Auntie, I just deliver them. Keri-mean?

GRANNY   No.

**FISH
SELLER**   Filopia?

GRANNY   No.

**FISH
SELLER**   Shrimp is there.

GRANNY   Smelts?

**FISH
SELLER**   No.

GRANNY   Pomfret?

> *The FISH SELLER clicks his tongue: Tisk'tisk.*

What else you have?

FISH SELLER The net catches what it catches Auntie.

GRANNY Not today.

FISH SELLER Don't go Auntie. Take a look.

GRANNY Come back tomorrow. Bring kingfish. Big ones.

FISH SELLER Small ones are tastier Grandma.

GRANNY I'm not a young woman. Stop your nonsense.

FISH SELLER Try, buy, you'll like.

GRANNY I'm going.

FISH SELLER Pay me tomorrow.

GRANNY I'm going inside.

FISH SELLER Show your sons. Go get them.

GRANNY They're not here. Goodbye.

FISH SELLER Go bring them.

GRANNY They're not here.

FISH SELLER Ask them.

GRANNY Stop bothering – you're bothering too much!

*GRANNY exits into the house. SERVANT GIRL
quickly follows. The FISHSELLER re-packs his fish
in newspaper but leaves one on the porch. He speaks to
TOMMY aloft in the tree.*

**FISH
SELLER**   The coalition government got me a new bicycle seat.
Next month when the communists come to power
I will get my own store with a refrigerator. I won't
have to hurry when I work, afraid my fish will spoil.
I will sit in my little store and you people will come
to me.

Pause.

Boy. Who are you?

*GRANNY returns, pouring coffee from one glass to
another to cool then gives it to the FISHSELLER.*

**FISH
SELLER**   Pray for a majority government. God listens to old
women.

GRANNY   In a few weeks we'll need lots of fish.

**FISH
SELLER**   Are you dying?

GRANNY   Not a funeral. A wedding.

**FISH
SELLER**   You're getting married Grandma?

GRANNY   Tina.

**FISH
SELLER**   Have you found the husband?

GRANNY   There's a boy in the city. My sons are meeting the
family in a few days.

FISHSELLER hands the coffee back to GRANNY.

**FISH
SELLER**   Please Grandma – not today. My stomach is paining
again.

GRANNY   See you tomorrow.

**FISH
SELLER**   Maybe I'll come.
BUY BUY!
FRESH BIG FISH!
BUY BUY!
FRESH BIG FISH!

> *FISHSELLER rings his bicycle bell as he rides away.*

**SERVANT
GIRL**   *(shouts at the FISHSELLER)* If you were still my husband, you'd wear nice shirts!

GRANNY   Take your fish.

> *The SERVANT GIRL takes the fish left for her on the
porch and follows GRANNY into the house.*

Scene: India
—•—•—

> *FATHER sits on the front porch spitting red beetle nut
juice into a cup. TOMMY enters and climbs the tree.*

TOMMY   I see you.

FATHER   I see you too.

TOMMY   No I see you. You always leave the house.

FATHER   Tina's wedding. Uncle needs help.

TOMMY   Auntie says I shouldn't say anything. I see you go to
the river. Why you throw rocks at the water? Why
you cry?

FATHER   Walk on my back. I'll give you some money.

TOMMY climbs down the tree.

TOMMY   How much?

FATHER   Five rupees.

TOMMY   I saw you crying.

FATHER   Do something. My back hurts.

TOMMY   Stop sleeping on the floor at night.

FATHER   I don't fit in the bed anymore. It's the same one I had when I was a boy.

> *TOMMY steps onto his FATHER's back but doesn't walk.*

TOMMY   Granny wants us to stay longer.

FATHER   We can't. You have school.

TOMMY   Only in September.

FATHER   We can't. Why are you asking? You don't like it here.

> *TOMMY continues standing still.*

What you do, you just sit and watch me all day? You should play with Tina. Walk.

> *TOMMY steps off of his FATHER.*

TOMMY   *(holding his hand out)* The money.

FATHER   Ask Granny.

TOMMY   I'll take your matches instead.

FATHER   Matches aren't for children.

> *FATHER gives TOMMY a box of matches. UNCLE runs onto the porch from the street.*

UNCLE	It was amazing. The bus was driving then it turned and hit the pole. We pushed forward then fell back. It was quiet for a moment then screaming. The children and a goat. It stumbled up and down the aisle, one of its legs was broken. The bus was tilted on its side and we moved forward, climbing over the seats. The driver wasn't drunk. He was dead. Heart attack. We were near the medial centre – some of us ran to get a doctor, some stayed back. Running, running out of breath. We got back and the bus was empty. The driver's fingers were chopped off. Blood all over the steering and the dash. He was just sitting there in his underwear. That goat shit bus. They took everything. Rings, necklace, even his socks. The doctor went back to his hospital. I came back here. An ugly ugly sight. I hope you never have to see something like that. You want to go see? It's still there.

FATHER eagerly stands to join his brother. TINA slides onto the front porch.

TINA	Did you get a new tie?
UNCLE	My God – I left it on the bus.
FATHER	Wait, let me put on a shirt.

FATHER runs inside the house to get a shirt.

TOMMY	You want me to tell you what it looks like?
TINA	No.
TOMMY	I licked a cow.
TINA	No you didn't.

FATHER returns holding a shirt.

FATHER	Come, come.
TOMMY	Be careful.

FATHER runs past TOMMY, exiting with UNCLE.

TINA   Why didn't you go with them? I would.

          TOMMY follows FATHER and UNCLE.

Scene: Canada
—•—•—

          *TOMMY wanders the countryside with his milk
          carton. He meets a Mennonite FARMER.*

FARMER   Who are you?

TOMMY   You're a Mennonite. You wear black and don't believe
          in electricity.

FARMER   I've never seen a brown fella before.

          *TOMMY preens as the FARMER inspects him up
          close.*

TOMMY   A lady from church gave me an ostrich egg. I almost
          hatched it but I sat on it too hard. When I see nice
          pictures in a magazine, I eat them. I steal jam from
          the grocery store and drop the bottles from the bridge
          near our house.

FARMER   I sat in a car once. No one knew.

TOMMY   At lunchtime the children chase me round the school-
          house with a skipping rope and try to hang me from a
          tree. It's because my father's from India. He used to
          be a math professor. He'd figure out problems on the
          wallpaper in the kitchen but then he got fired. He
          took me to India last summer. He wanted to get a job
          there but it wasn't like he remembered. Now he works
          for Mother's Pizza. People think I talk to myself but
          there's someone there.

          TOMMY points to the sky.

          I see the counsellor every morning but she hasn't fixed
          me yet. My teacher says I'm retarded. I like it better
          high up.

> *TOMMY races up a tree by the side of the road.*

FARMER   What do you see?

TOMMY   A big field. Snow.

FARMER   What else?

TOMMY   That's all.

FARMER   No, keep looking. I was born on this farm, that house right there. My whole life, I've never gone past that road.

> *Silence.*

What do you see?

> *Silence.*

It's my tree.

> *TOMMY returns to the ground.*

Where do you live?

TOMMY   Kitchener.

FARMER   You should go. Your parents must be worried.

TOMMY   They're all gone. My mother drowned 10 years ago when we went to India. She went swimming in the river behind the house where she grew up. She swam there everyday when she was a girl but she forgot where the dangerous spots were. They never found her body. She sunk to the bottom but my father doesn't know for sure. Which way to Kitchener?

> *The Mennonite FARMER points. TOMMY starts walking in the opposite direction.*

FARMER   You're going the wrong way. You're headed toward St. Jacobs.

TOMMY	I went to India last summer. I'm never going back.

> *TOMMY starts running. The Mennonite FARMER crosses to the tree, climbs up and starts to gaze.*

Scene: India
—•—•—

> *TOMMY and UNCLE enter as TINA sits on the porch.*

TOMMY	It was amazing. You want me to tell you?
TINA	No.

> *Silence.*

TOMMY	I really licked a cow before.
TINA	No you didn't.
TOMMY	I did. This morning your father was going to milk it and I was on the other side. It was moaning and moving its feet. I leaned on it and the hair scratched my face. It smelled like a soccer ball and my cheek pumped into my teeth. Uncle told me to "Listen–
UNCLE	*(overlapping, interrupting)* "Listen to the stomach."
TOMMY	I put my ear where he pointed.
UNCLE	*(interrupting)* The inside was exploding. Like the lakes that boil before sunset. "Damn thing's been into the sugar cane again."
TOMMY	The cow kicked at air as we moved around for more sounds.
UNCLE	*(interrupting)* I took a big knife,
TOMMY	The one he uses to split open the coconuts then–

UNCLE   (*interrupting*) I push it into the cow's stomach then I pull it back out. The smell. But the cow stops shaking. It feels better. I take string and stitch up the skin like a doctor.

UNCLE exits.

TOMMY   I really licked the cow.

TINA   How do I know you're telling the truth?

TOMMY   It tasted the way dirty underwear smells. Anything you want, I can do. Think of something.

TINA   No.

TOMMY   Think.

TINA   Some night, you should steal a sari from my mother's closet. I want you to go to the station and tie it to the back of a bus.

TOMMY   I'll make it drag on the road, all the way out of town.

TINA   Did you go to the ocean yesterday?

TOMMY   Yes. With my father.

TINA   What was it like? Tell me.

TOMMY   We lay on the sand eating cashews and jackfruit. We drank mango juice quickly before it dried in our cup. I didn't like it. Father said it tasted better when he was little. We lay against the boats that were turned over to dry out. Only mad dogs and Englishmen out at this hour but Father wanted me to see all the fishermen when they come in. Up to keep cool. Chasing the water then turning and running back. My father picks me up and throws me back in. The two of us stand strong against the water trying not to fall over. Over and over the waves shake us. I turn to grab onto him but there's nothing to hold onto. Put your clothes back on! I shout. Looking back to the beach. Shirts, shorts, underwear, empty on the sand.

Stripped by the ocean but we didn't even realize.
We didn't see any boats. Uncle told us they go to
a different beach now.

TINA   Run through the sugar cane. Pull water from the well.
Will you tell me what it feels like to walk in the rice
paddies?

TOMMY   I'll go for you.

TINA   My life will change when I get married. I will finally
leave this house.

TOMMY   I can take you to the bus station. You can tie the sari.

TINA   What?

TOMMY   One night. When the others are sleeping we can go to
the city. I'll roll you.

TINA   How?

TOMMY   We can go after prayers.

TINA   No one will know?

>   *TOMMY shakes his head.*

My life on this patio has been so small. I've never
been afraid of anything.

TOMMY   You don't have to wait until you get married.

>   *Beat.*

I'll be the husband.

Scene: India
—•—•—

>   *TOMMY runs through the fields.*

TOMMY   I run through the sugar cane. I pull water from the
well. I'm walking in the rice paddies. I stand in the

water and the minnows and tadpoles nibble at the hair
on my legs. The rice plants scratch like puppy's teeth.
The roots wrap around my ankles and I sink into the
mudsuck up to my shins. The water snakes come close
and I have to splash my hands to keep them away.
I try to step but the mud doesn't let go. Stuck deep
until the Fishseller pulls me free.

Scene: India
—•—•—

*GRANNY, AUNTIE, and the SERVANT GIRL,
wash clothes by the river, slapping them against rocks.
Their saris are rolled up to the knee. Barefeet. Water
splashes. They stop, inspect their work, then slap again.
Over and over, start then stop. Rhythmic music.*

AUNTIE   A man's shirt. Easier than a sari.

*SERVANT GIRL trades with AUNTIE, giving
her the sari and taking the man's shirt. She leads in
the washing, slapping harder than the others do.
GRANNY and AUNTIE stop to watch her violent
solo.*

**SERVANT
GIRL**   My body feels wonderful.

Scene: India
—•—•—

The porch. UNCLE and FATHER smoke beadies.

UNCLE   Where's Tina?

FATHER   Inside.

UNCLE   Where's the boy?

FATHER   I don't know. What is it you want to say?

UNCLE	After Tina gets married, my wife is going to leave this house.
FATHER	Brother. You talk nonsense.
UNCLE	Long time ago, my wife would bring lunch to me at the talcum factory. In the big room the men smash rocks into powder. We all look the same in the dust – gray. I would stand quiet and make my wife find me by my smell, my sweat. She'd move among the men, smelling at the neck until I was there. We would eat fish curry and rice from the tifin carrier, the spices lifting into our face, stinging the tongue. I touch her nose with mine, roll one way against her face then roll the other way, leaving a white mask on her skin. But then she stopped bringing me food. When my wife makes love she grips the head of our bed. I dusted powder onto the wood one morning before I left for work. I came back in the evening and saw the marks of her fingers. I walked into the pepper field behind our house and lay on the ground until I could stand up again.

Beat.

	Tina was born. Our mother moved into our house. My wife was no longer alone during the day. She started bringing me lunch again. Just as before.
FATHER	Who was the man?
UNCLE	Our doctor. I go to him when I'm sick. He looks into my eyes. He touches my body. All these years he's made me feel better.
FATHER	Get a new doctor.
UNCLE	He's the best in the village. He lives close by. He knows our family. My wife will go to him after the wedding. Don't cry.
FATHER	Your pain is as big as mine.

UNCLE   I still kiss my wife. Lightly on the shoulder when she sleeps.

> *Silence.*

A place changes. But you still see what it was before. Maybe I will stay here. Maybe I will move away. I don't know.

> *Beat.*

I want you to listen. This boy for Tina. We'll see him tomorrow. May God give us a wedding.

Scene: India
—•—•—

> *TOMMY runs through a sugarcane field.*

TOMMY   How can I describe what this feels like? The sugarcane grass is so high all I see is green. This green is darker than the leaves on the coconut tree but lighter than the frogs that come onto the porch at night to cool off.

> *Gazes silently at the sugarcane grass surrounding him.*

Some things can't be described.

Scene: India
—•—•—

> *Evening prayers. GRANNY, FATHER, UNCLE, AUNTIE, TINA, and SERVANT GIRL sit on straw mats. AUNTIE holds the bible and reads passages from the Songs of Solomon. The bible is passed around.*

AUNTIE   My lover is an apple tree. The finest in the orchard. I am seated in his much-desired shade and his fruit is lovely to eat.

FATHER   He brings me to the banquet hall and everyone can see how much he loves me.

> *TOMMY enters and is slapped on the head by his father for being late.*

Oh feed me with your love – your raisins and your apples, for I am utterly lovesick. His left hand is under my head and with his right hand he embraces me.

TINA   Ah, I hear him, my beloved! Here he comes, leaping upon the mountains and bounding over the hills. My beloved is like a gazelle or young deer. Look, there he is behind the wall now, looking in at the windows.

GRANNY   *(simultaneously with TINA, from memory)* Look. There he is behind the wall now, looking in at the windows.

UNCLE   My beloved says to me, "Rise up, my love, my fair one, and come away. For the winter is past and the rain is gone. The flowers are springing up and the time of the singing of the birds has come. Yes, spring is here. Arise my fair one and come away."

TINA   How sweet is your love my darling, my bride. How much better it is than mere white wine. The perfume of your love is more fragrant than all the richest spices. Your lips, my dear are made of honey.

FATHER   Read Tommy–

TOMMY   Yes, honey and cream are under your tongue, and the scent of your garments is like the scent of the mountains and cedars of Lebanon.

> *SERVANT GIRL sighs. Blackout. The always-present power strikes. Voices in the dark.*

FATHER   *(v/o, curses)* Che! Electric Company Fucks!

AUNTIE   *(v/o)* Pray Tommy.

SERVANT GIRL	*(v/o)* Should I go?
GRANNY	*(v/o)* Wait. Let's see.

Pause. No light.

SERVANT GIRL	*(v/o)* Should I go?
GRANNY	*(v/o)* Wait.
AUNTIE	*(v/o)* Pray Tommy.
SERVANT GIRL	*(v/o)* I'll go.
AUNTIE	*(v/o)* Yes. Go get the flashlight.
TOMMY	*(v/o)* I'll go.
FATHER	*(v/o)* Wait here.
AUNTIE	*(v/o)* Granny?
GRANNY	*(v/o)* Right here.
UNCLE	*(v/o)* What's this?
AUNTIE	*(v/o)* What?
UNCLE	*(v/o)* Who's this?
AUNTIE	*(v/o)* What?
UNCLE	*(v/o)* Who's this? Who am I touching?
AUNTIE	*(v/o)* Your wife.
UNCLE	*(v/o)* I'm sorry.
FATHER	*(v/o)* How much longer?
GRANNY	*(v/o)* Don't get up.

TOMMY   *(v/o)* You don't have to hold my foot.

AUNTIE   *(v/o)* Pray Tommy.

TOMMY   *(v/o)* What for?

Sound of a slap.

FATHER   *(v/o)* Just pray. Don't get smart.

GRANNY   *(v/o)* Don't get up.

TOMMY   *(v/o)* Owww! Shit.

SERVANT GIRL   *(v/o)* Sorry.

SERVANT GIRL returns with a weak oil lamp.

TOMMY   *(v/o)* Who stepped on my hand?

AUNTIE   *(v/o)* Pray for Tina. Pray for the wedding.

GRANNY   *(v/o)* Pray Tina.

UNCLE   *(v/o)* Big girl.

Silence.

GRANNY   *(v/o)* Tina?

AUNTIE   *(v/o)* What?

GRANNY   *(v/o)* Where's Tina?

TOMMY   *(v/o)* Let go of my foot.

AUNTIE   *(v/o)* That's my foot.

GRANNY   *(v/o)* Where's Tina then?

UNCLE   *(v/o)* Tina?

FATHER   *(v/o)* Where could she go?

AUNTIE   *(v/o)* Tina!

GRANNY   *(v/o)* Tina girl!

> *Lights up as electricity returns. TINA sits quietly.*

AUNTIE   You heard us talking.

GRANNY   Tina–

AUNTIE   When we say something Tina, talk back. Don't just sit there.

TINA   I don't want to talk.

TOMMY   She's just quiet.

AUNTIE   Quiet Tommy.

UNCLE   You're getting married but I can still slap you.

AUNTIE   Go for a walk. I'll make you a tea when you get back.

> *Blackout.*

FATHER   *(v/o, curses)* Che-da! Fucksake!

AUNTIE   *(v/o)* Pray Tommy.

UNCLE   *(v/o)* Tina?

> *Silence.*

(v/o) Tina?

> *Silence.*

(v/o) Say something Tina.

TINA   *(v/o)* You can stop. I hear you.

AUNTIE   *(v/o)* Good girl.

Scene: Canada
—•—•—

Evening. TOMMY wanders the streets and reads the milk carton:

TOMMY Doug Harris. St. Jacobs Ontario. 12 years old. Blond hair. Blue eyes. 4 feet 8 inches. 100 pounds. Last seen September 1974.

TOMMY opens the milk carton and pours its contents onto his snowsuit:

Milk Boy.

Scene: India
—•—•—

Night. GRANNY sleeps in her bed. The SERVANT GIRL sits on the floor in the bedroom doorway beside an oil lamp, brushing her long hair. She lies on her mat and turns off the oil lamp. Few beats. The oil lamp comes on again. The SERVANT GIRL sits and continues combing her hair. She stops to smell the brush.

Sccne: India
—•—•—

In the city. The NUTSELLER sits in the street. TINA sits on her cart as TOMMY stands alongside. TINA ties a beautiful red sari to the bumper of a bus.

NUT SELLER Sweet sweet. Sweet Nuts. Sweet sweet. Sweet Nuts. Sweet sweet. Sweet Nuts.

TOMMY Did you tie it tight?

TINA I don't want to let go. I want to hold on and get pulled away.

TOMMY In Canada I hold onto the back of the school bus when it snows and I slide on my boots.

TINA	I've never seen these many people in one place.
TOMMY	This is really the first time you've left your house?
TINA	This is the first time I remember. My parents carried me around when I was a baby but then I got big and had to stay home.
NUT SELLER	Sweet sweet. Sweet Nuts. Sweet sweet. Sweet Nuts.
TOMMY	What else do you want to do, Wife?
TINA	I want to do everything, Husband.
TOMMY	We have to be back before the others wake up.
TINA	I don't want to practice the rice pattern anymore. I want to go down that street.
TOMMY	Have you ever tasted beer?
TINA	No.
TOMMY	I want to.
TINA	Buy from that man. He'll sell you one.
TOMMY	You want one?
TINA	No. There's a restaurant. The Anjali. I want to go there and have a milkshake in a big glass.
TOMMY	What flavour?
TINA	Doesn't matter.
TOMMY	You've never had a milkshake?
TINA	I have. But not in a big glass. All the glasses at home are little.
NUT SELLER	Sweet sweet. Sweet Nuts. Sweet sweet. Sweet Nuts.

TOMMY	We can come back tomorrow. Every night until you get married. Tie your shoes Wife.

TOMMY bends to tie TINA's shoes.

TINA	Don't touch – I can do it.

TINA ties her own shoes.

Show your hands. Your fingers are yellow.

TOMMY	I helped Granny pick curry leaves.

TOMMY pushes the cart as TINA shines a flashlight to light their way. The girl drags her hand on the ground, erasing the marks of their travels.

In Canada, I pick blueberries for Mr. Timlock. You could come back with me and make lots of money. He gives me a quarter a carton. I put milk bags over my shoes to keep the mud off. You have to be careful when you hand your baskets in at the end of the day. Rinse your mouth or he'll see the purple on your teeth Your hands are filthy.

TINA	This way no one can find us. Are your arms tired?
TOMMY	No.
TINA	I can push myself. I only need help when we get home. The hill up to our house is too hard.
NUT SELLER	Sweet sweet. Sweet Nuts.

TOMMY starts to spin in circles.

TINA	What are you doing?

Tommy continues to spin.

Tommy!

TOMMY stops spinning and falls to the ground.

TOMMY   I'm dizzy. Everything's going in circles.

TINA   Why?

TOMMY   Because I'm dizzy.

TINA   What's dizzy?

> *TOMMY spins TINA on her cart. Both collapse on the ground.*

I'm dizzy.

TOMMY   No more India.

**NUT
SELLER**   Sweet sweet. Sweet Nuts.

> *TINA sets herself back on her cart. TOMMY staggers to his feet.*

TOMMY   You want to wait until the bus drives away so you can watch?

TINA   No, I want to see more. Let's go to the cinema.

TOMMY   We should be careful. Indira Gandhi steals people at night and gives them operations so they don't have children.

TINA   She won't do that to us. Just the poor people.

> *TINA wheels herself away.*

Get a branch. Rub our marks off the ground.

> *TOMMY follows behind dragging his feet, erasing their trail.*

**NUT
SELLER**   Sweet sweet. Sweet Nuts. Sweet sweet. Sweet Nuts.

Scene: Canada
—•—•—

*FATHER continues to sleep on the kitchen counter.
GRANNY whispers in his ear:*

GRANNY   A nightmare: The handsome man and his beautiful
wife go to the river to swim but only one returns to
shore. People hear you screaming and come running
with flashlights. You cover yourself with one hand and
with the other you point to where you last saw your
wife. The men dive deep as you crawl in the dark
trying to find your pants. The women wrap you in
your wife's sari then sit in the dirt with you until
morning. Your clothes hang in the tree where you left
them. You change. Your beautiful wife is never found.
She sunk to the bottom of the river. Or was carried to
the sea. Or did she just swim away? Is she in Cape
Comoran eating beef biriyani in a five-star? Is she in
Mysore sucking on a mango seed as she swings in a
hammock? Your beautiful wife walks in the Nilgris
wiping the soap from another man's ear. The two of
them talk about the problems in your marriage when
they stop kissing. Your wife always cut the top of
your head off when using a camera so you took the
pictures. Every photo in the house is of her. You hide
them in a box downstairs. Years later your pipes burst.
The basement floods. You stand knee deep in water as
your wife floats on the surface – hundreds of pictures.
She smiles up at you as you worry about the carpet.

    Beat.

You lost your wife. Go find your son.

    *GRANNY exits. FATHER wakes, goes to the window,
and looks up into the tree.*

FATHER   Tommy? Are you there? Hul-lo. Hul-lo. Hul-lo sir.

Scene: India
—•—•—

*Early morning. TOMMY wheels TINA from the
street toward the front porch.*

TOMMY   We're late.

TINA   Doesn't matter.

TOMMY   Granny's going to be waiting with the rice.

TINA   She can do the pattern. I'm tired.

TOMMY   Talk softly. What should we tell her?

TOMMY and TINA enter the porch.

TOMMY   Where is she?

*TOMMY enters the house. GRANNY enters the porch
behind TINA. She, too, has been out during the night.*

TINA   Granny! What were you doing?

GRANNY   You know what I was doing.

TINA   I won't say anything.

GRANNY   I'm going to bed.

TINA   You want me to do the rice pattern?

GRANNY   I walked all over the city looking for my husband.
Calling his name, getting upset but then I found him.
All is better. He has a place in the cemetery.

Scene: Canada
—•—•—

*Evening. TOMMY stands in front of a door then rings
the bell. MR. HARRIS opens the door.*

TOMMY   Mr. Harris. I don't have blond hair or blue eyes. I'm taller than 4 feet 8 inches and bigger than 100 pounds but I can be your son. I'll shine your shoes Sunday mornings if you wake me up. I'll shovel the porch if you do the drive. I'll dry if you wash. All you have to do is feed me and take me for rides in the car wash. I'll be proud to eat with you at the A&W instead of making you do drive-thru. People won't stare at us when we buy our groceries at Zehr's. You won't talk with an accent. You'll teach me how to throw a spiral. You'll do oil changes in the driveway. This driveway. It's been more than a year. I don't think Doug is coming back.

MR. HARRIS   Come inside.

    TOMMY enters the house.

Scene: India
—•—•—

    Dusk. A soccer field. FATHER and UNCLE in shirt and tie play soccer. TOMMY follows from behind also in shirt and tie. The men are drunk from toddy made with coconut milk. They drink from coconut shells. TOMMY is sober.

UNCLE   Nice house.

FATHER   Nice car.

UNCLE   Nice wife.

FATHER   Nice daughters.

UNCLE   Nice Alsation.

FATHER   A very Christian family.

UNCLE   None more so–

FATHER   Very important.

UNCLE	Very important.
FATHER	We share the same values.
UNCLE	Definitely. Kick.

> *FATHER kicks the ball weakly to UNCLE.*

FATHER	How long have you been looking?
UNCLE	A few months maybe.
FATHER	He's a nice boy.
UNCLE	Pass.

> *FATHER passes the soccer ball.*

FATHER	A quiet boy. Strange.

> *TOMMY suddenly disappears. He has fallen into a ground-level well.*

Like Tina.

UNCLE	He's better. He went to school. He can't run but he can walk.
FATHER	They'll be happy. I hope so.
UNCLE	All we can do is try.
TOMMY	*(v/o)* Dad!
FATHER	The boy didn't smile.
UNCLE	His mind is fine.
FATHER	He didn't say anything.
UNCLE	He can talk.
TOMMY	*(v/o)* Dad!

FATHER   I worry.

UNCLE   We'll live close by. We'll watch over.

FATHER   Who was that man in the kitchen?

UNCLE   The one with a red tie?

FATHER   Him. Yes.

TOMMY   *(v/o)* Hey!

UNCLE   It's not who you think.

TOMMY   *(v/o)* Hey!

FATHER   Who do I think?

UNCLE   You think the bad luck tailor.

FATHER   Yes! The bad luck tailor. I remember the bad luck tailor. There is still the bad luck tailor!

UNCLE   If he says hello to you, a bus hits you. He told the butcher he liked his haircut. The poor man doesn't leave the house for a week. He finally goes to work, the first day back he cuts off his thumb.

FATHER   Don't look at him,

UNCLE   Don't shake his hand,

FATHER   Don't scratch his dog,

UNCLE   Don't pinch his wife,

FATHER   Don't let her pinch you,

UNCLE   He brings bad luck wherever he goes.

FATHER   He's part of our family now? Fools.

FATHER falls to the ground.

UNCLE   No, no. I thought so too, but we're lucky. That was one of the boy's uncles. He just looks like the bad luck tailor.

FATHER   The bad luck tailor is still alive.

UNCLE   Still downtown.

           Beat.

           Don't go to his store. Never.

FATHER   How does he survive?

UNCLE   We put money under his door so he doesn't drop by.

           Silence.

           Is this marriage a good thing?

FATHER   This is good.

UNCLE   I don't want to go home.

FATHER   I should've never come back.

UNCLE   You were happy when you got here.

FATHER   The great math professor.

UNCLE   Come back to India.

FATHER   Why?

UNCLE   You can teach at the college.

FATHER   There is nothing for me here.

UNCLE   You can live with me. In my empty house.

FATHER   You come to Canada. My empty house.

UNCLE   If we're going to talk like this then no more talking.

Silence.

No more toddy.

> *UNCLE puts the empty coconut shell on his head.*
> *FATHER does the same.*

FATHER   More drink Tommy.

UNCLE   Where's the boy?

FATHER   Dammit.

UNCLE   What's wrong?

FATHER   He's hiding. Tommy! I'm too drunk.

UNCLE   Where is he?

FATHER   Hiding. Tommy!

UNCLE   Where are you boy?

FATHER   Tommy!

UNCLE   Tommy!

FATHER   Tommy!

UNCLE   Nephew!

FATHER   Nephew!

> *They come upon the well.*

FATHER   Tommy?

> *FATHER and UNCLE peer into the depths.*

UNCLE   Do you see anything?

FATHER   Are those eyes?

UNCLE   I can't see.

FATHER   Tommy?

TOMMY   I fell in the well.

UNCLE   –My God,

FATHER   Are you hurt?

TOMMY   No.

FATHER   Is it deep?

TOMMY   No.

FATHER   You're okay. We'll get some rope.

> *FATHER and UNCLE collapse to the ground.*
> *TOMMY climbs out of the well.*

Scene: India
—•—•—

> *The FISHSELLER walks his bicycle calling out for customers.*

FISH SELLER   BUY BUY!
FRESH BIG FISH!

> *The SERVANT GIRL enters and sees the FISH SELLER – both stop.*

Yes, hello.

SERVANT GIRL   Fine, how are you?

FISH SELLER   Yes, how are you?

SERVANT GIRL   Good, how are you?

**FISH
SELLER**   I'm glad.

Silence.

My new bicycle seat. It's too hard. My body aches when I work.

Beat.

It will get better.

FISHSELLER exits.

Scene: India
—•—•—

TINA practices her design on the porch. TOMMY enters.

TOMMY   I met your husband. You're not pretty but still. He's terrible.

Silence.

What do you want to know?

Silence.

TINA   Can he walk?

TOMMY   Yes.

TINA   Does he have hands?

TOMMY   Yes.

TINA   I'll make him pull me like I make you.

UNCLE enters the porch.

UNCLE   The boy is like you. Quiet. His face is ugly but his hands are nice. You'll have children. Don't worry. They

won't come through you. The doctor will cut them
from your stomach like he cut you from your mother.
Your children will be better than you. Strong. Healthy.
Smart. They'll take care of you. I'm going to sleep.

UNCLE exits.

TINA   Where should we go tonight?

TOMMY   I don't care.

TINA   I'm tired of downtown.

TOMMY   Then don't go. I'll go by myself.

TINA   We should take the train and go to Madras. Or
Cochin. I want to read the news on state television.
Every day the producers drive around Kerala and pick
a different girl. Why not me? My face is pretty
enough. You wouldn't see my legs behind the desk.
I'm going to wander the streets until I get picked.

TOMMY   You need me. I could trick you and leave you in the
city. You'd get in so much trouble.

TINA   So would you.

TOMMY   Not as much as you – you're older. I'd tell them you
made me take you and that you didn't want to come
home.

TINA   You wouldn't do that. You like me too much.

TOMMY   I'm not going to tell you when, but one night I'm just
going to leave you there.

GRANNY   Leave her.

*TOMMY enters the house. GRANNY steps onto the
porch.*

Don't worry, Tommy will be gone in a few weeks. You
have to get married Tina.

Scene: Canada
—•—•—

St. Jacobs. TOMMY lies in Doug Harris' bed. MR.
HARRIS sits beside him, eyes closed.

TOMMY   You want me to tell you a bedtime story?

MR.
HARRIS   No.

TOMMY   I can't sleep.

MR.
HARRIS   Try.

TOMMY   Where's my mother?

MR.
HARRIS   She's not here anymore.

TOMMY   Did she die?

MR.
HARRIS   We're divorced. Stop talking.

TOMMY   Open your eyes.

MR.
HARRIS   I repainted the whole house. I did the basement and
the kitchen and the family room – but I got upstairs
and couldn't do your room. Can you smell the paint
from downstairs?

TOMMY   What do you do?

MR.
HARRIS   I work for Kitchener Hydro. I go into people's
backyards to read the meter. I looked in hundreds
of windows to see if you were inside. I don't want to
know where you've been. Never tell me. You're back
now, that's all that matters.

TOMMY rolls over.

No – Doug sleeps on his back.

TOMMY   Turn on the lights. I'm not tired yet.

**MR.
HARRIS**   You can't keep talking.

TOMMY   Let's do something. Let's go outside.

**MR.
HARRIS**   No.

TOMMY   We can look at the Christmas lights.

**MR.
HARRIS**   I wasn't going to put them up this year but I forced
myself. Yes. Let's go outside and look. Promise not to
talk?

No response.

Good boy.

Scene: India

—•—•—

*SERVANT GIRL carries two buckets of water. TINA
follows, dragging herself on the ground. SERVANT
GIRL rolls up her sari and TINA disrobes.
SERVANT GIRL wets TINA's hair, dipping
a plastic cup into the bucket.*

**SERVANT
GIRL**   Your hair isn't as nice as mine. Mine's thicker. I have
beautiful hair. Clean. No smell. Everybody tells me.
I walk in the town and the shopkeepers beg me to cut
it off. They'll give me lots of money. Close your eyes.

SERVANT GIRL starts to lather.

Che! I forgot the towel. Wait here.

SERVANT GIRL exits. TOMMY enters. He's been watching from the bushes. TINA's eyes are still closed. TOMMY starts to shampoo. TINA immediately opens her eyes and turns, discovering her cousin is washing her hair. She covers her breasts and lets him continue. TOMMY lifts TINA's hands in his and brings them to her head – the two lather her hair. Both are transfixed. TOMMY reaches for the plastic cup to rinse, but TINA hands him the shampoo bottle – she wants more. Sound of SERVANT GIRL approaching. TOMMY runs away.

SERVANT GIRL　　Good girl. All by yourself.

Scene: India
—•—•—

An umbrella repairman sits in the street. TOMMY approaches in shorts.

TOMMY　　How much to fix?

UMBRELLAMAN inspects TOMMY's umbrella for repair.

UMBRELLA MAN　　You have nice legs.

TOMMY　　Thank you. I think it's the spring.

UMBRELLA MAN　　Maybe. Yes. It's the spring.

TOMMY　　How long will it take to fix?

UMBRELLA MAN　　No time. Wait.

UMBRELLAMAN works.

Like a girl's. You shave them?

TOMMY   No.

**UMBRELLA
MAN**   I love these legs.

TOMMY   Your hands are greasy!

**UMBRELLA
MAN**   It's good you brought your umbrella in. The floods
will start soon.

TOMMY   How much will this cost?

**UMBRELLA
MAN**   25 rupees.

TOMMY   10.

**UMBRELLA
MAN**   10 Boy!

TOMMY   My Granny said 10.

**UMBRELLA
MAN**   15.

TOMMY   My Granny gave me 10.

**UMBRELLA
MAN**   Get more.

TOMMY   5.

**UMBRELLA
MAN**   5 now!

TOMMY   5 and you can feel my legs.

> *Silence.*

**UMBRELLA
MAN**   Naughty boy. Okay.

> *UMBRELLA MAN caresses TOMMY's legs.*

TOMMY   How much for your whistle?

> *TOMMY points to a whistle around UMBRELLA MAN's neck.*

UMBRELLA MAN   10 rupees.

TOMMY   5.

UMBRELLA MAN   5 and you feel my legs.

TOMMY   What?

UMBRELLA MAN   Feel my legs.

TOMMY   Give me the whistle.

> *UMBRELLAMAN hands TOMMY the whistle. The boy blows.*

UMBRELLA MAN   It works.

> *The boy blows the whistle again.*

Feel.

> *UMBRELLAMAN stretches out his legs and closes his eyes. TOMMY rubs, intermittently blowing the whistle.*

Scene: Canada
—•—•—

> *Exterior. TOMMY stands in front of a tree. MR. HARRIS calls from off-stage:*

MR. HARRIS   *(v/o)* Close your eyes Doug. Ready?

> *The Christmas lights come on. They shine oddly, the string of lights only placed halfway up the tree. MR. HARRIS joins TOMMY.*

Just like we always do. It was hard doing it by myself.

TOMMY   *(whispers)* Looks dumb.

MR. HARRIS   I couldn't go higher – you weren't here to hold the ladder.

> *MR. HARRIS exits and returns with a ladder.*

Hold the ladder.

TOMMY   I want to climb up.

MR. HARRIS   You can't be my son if you're going to keep talking. You don't sound like Doug so just hold the ladder.

> *TOMMY holds the ladder. MR. HARRIS climbs up to extend the lights higher in the tree. He returns to the ground.*

You want to climb up? I'll hold. Go on. You can see Kitchener. The library. K-Mart. Canada Trust.

> *TOMMY climbs to the top and looks toward Kitchener.*

Tomorrow we'll go to the Farmer's Market. Haven't been there for a while. I'll buy a tray of apple fritters and we can go to the Siskin's game. After the hockey we'll have cheeseburgers at Harmony Lunch. Our clothes will smell like fried onions. For supper we'll do the buffet at Mei King or wiener schnitzel at the Schwaben Club. Stupid me, eh, I forgot – the Father-Son Christmas dinner is this weekend at church – you came back just in time. Everyone will be there. They'll be surprised to see you.

> *Silence.*

Maybe you should come down.

TOMMY climbs down the ladder.

For a few moments you made me feel better. Thank you. You should leave.

MR. HARRIS folds up the ladder and exits, leaving TOMMY standing by the lit up tree.

TOMMY   You're welcome. Where should I go?

TOMMY stands in the dark as MR. HARRIS unplugs the Christmas lights.

Scene: India
—•—•—

Early morning. TINA designs a pattern on the porch.

AUNTIE   You look tired. Are you getting enough sleep?

TINA   Yes.

AUNTIE   You're getting better. Bend your fingers like this.

AUNTIE goes to the floor and starts to design.

It's hard to see what you're doing when you're so close. You have to look from above. You like what I'm doing? I would make such big patterns – I covered the whole porch. You need a wedding sari. This afternoon we'll go downtown to the sari stores. You've never left this house. Don't be scared.

TINA   I'm not.

AUNTIE   Good girl.

Scene: India
—•—•—

> *UNCLE and FATHER cradle TOMMY over the toilet so that he doesn't have to touch the seat.*

TOMMY   I'm flying. A crow. Look out below.

FATHER   The stink.

UNCLE   Are you finished?

TOMMY   One more.

UNCLE   Finished?

TOMMY   Okay.

> *Pause.*

Wipe please.

> *FATHER and UNCLE look at each other. Neither moves.*

Wipe please.
Wipe.
Wipe!
WIPE!

Scene: India
—•—•—

> *A sari store. A clerk works disinterestedly, casually throwing saris around TINA as AUNTIE and SERVANT GIRL instruct. TINA is bored.*

AUNTIE   That one.

SERVANT GIRL   No, that one.

AUNTIE   No.

SERVANT GIRL	That one.
CLERK	*(trying to find the sari that the women point to)* This?
AUNTIE	Higher – No – That one – Not that one, that one. This one–

> *AUNTIE reaches out and grabs the sari she wants.*

CLERK	Omigod!
SERVANT GIRL	*(to the CLERK)* You're wasting our time!

> *CLERK swirls more saris around TINA's shoulders.*

AUNTIE	No. Try that one.
SERVANT GIRL	No Auntie, not for a wedding.
AUNTIE	What then?
CLERK	This one.
SERVANT GIRL	Mine had thin gold lines. Give one like that.
AUNTIE	More colour.

> *CLERK throws brighter saris.*

AUNTIE	That's too much.

> *CLERK keeps throwing.*

AUNTIE	Too bright. Too bright.
SERVANT GIRL	No. No. Che – No!

        CLERK stops throwing and shrugs his shoulders.

AUNTIE   Bring all your red ones.

**SERVANT
GIRL**   Red with gold border.

        CLERK leaves.

AUNTIE   He's useless. How are you Tina?

TINA   Fine.

**SERVANT
GIRL**   You like the city?

TINA   Yes.

        CLERK returns with a stack of saris.

**SERVANT
GIRL**   Bring the bride some drink.

CLERK   You want chai?

AUNTIE   She's a child. Bring a soft drink.

CLERK   Limca, Thums Up, Campa Cola?

AUNTIE   Choose Tina.

TINA   Bring a Goldspot.

        CLERK leaves.

AUNTIE   You're quiet Tina.

        *SERVANT GIRL throws some saris around TINA,
        drowning the woman in colour.*

**SERVANT
GIRL**   Colour,
        Colour,
           Swim,
             Swirl,
                Drown.

Scene: Canada
—•—•—

> *Evening. Sound of thrashing. TOMMY is covered in dirt and husk. He has been running through a cornfield.*

TOMMY   I know where babies come from. I've got little seeds inside of me. I'm going to plant one in this cornfield. Come summer I'll have a baby. A new Tommy. Good Tommy. Canadian.

> *TOMMY falls to his knees and tries to dig a hole but can't. Angrily, he hits the frozen ground then unzips his trousers. He rubs into his hands, grinding against, but unable to penetrate, the soil. Face down, he finishes, wipes his hand in the snow, then repeatedly hits the ground. Then he lies still.*

Scene: India
—•—•—

> *The porch. SERVANT GIRL combs her hair as the FISHSELLER approaches.*

SERVANT GIRL   At night you would sleep with your fingers in my hair. My hair is clean now. No more fish smell.

> *Silence.*

Talk.

FISH SELLER   I have come for the wedding.

> *Both remain still.*

Scene: India

—•—•—

UNCLE and TOMMY in the backyard. UNCLE cleans his axe, his clothes covered in blood. TOMMY starts to gather up dead chickens.

TOMMY   This one's the winner. Look how far.

UNCLE   That one's still twitching.

TOMMY   He went running like this–

TOMMY runs a delirious, erratic zigzag.

UNCLE   You want to kill one?

TOMMY   Can I?

UNCLE hands TOMMY the axe – holds a chicken.

UNCLE   Quick and strong. Watch my fingers.

TOMMY   Count me down.

UNCLE   One, two, three – CHOP!

TOMMY   CHOP!

TOMMY swings the axe. UNCLE lets go of the chicken. The headless bird drops. No big run. AUNTIE enters, sees the execution and freezes, eyes-wide.

That's not fair. Mine didn't run.

UNCLE   Try again.

UNCLE holds another chicken.

One, two, three!

TOMMY swings the axe. Again the bird just drops.

TOMMY   Run! Do something!

TOMMY kicks the bird and UNCLE slaps TOMMY.

UNCLE   Show respect.

TOMMY   It should do something. It didn't even twitch.

UNCLE   Go wash.

TOMMY   We're not finished.

UNCLE   You have kidneys on your neck.

They notice frozen AUNTIE.

TOMMY   What's wrong with Auntie?

UNCLE   I didn't see her coming.

TOMMY   What's wrong?

UNCLE   She goes stiff if she sees an animal get hurt.

TOMMY   How long does she stay like this?

UNCLE   Not long – a few hours. Leave her. Pick up the chickens.

UNCLE stares at his wife.

So still. Beautiful.

TOMMY   Can she see us?

UNCLE   No.

TOMMY   Give her a kiss like Sleeping Beauty. You can be the prince. Wake her up.

UNCLE hesitates then kisses his wife on the lips. No reaction. She remains frozen.

I'll get the doctor.

UNCLE   No, she's fine. Help me.

>   *TOMMY helps him gather the dead birds.*

>   *SERVANT GIRL exits. FISHSELLER takes out a notebook. GRANNY enters. They go over final details.*

FISH SELLER   Kingfish Auntie.

GRANNY   Yes. How many will you bring?

FISH SELLER   Three hundred.

GRANNY   No.

FISH SELLER   Four?

GRANNY   Yes. And when will you bring them?

FISH SELLER   Tomorrow morning.

GRANNY   Good.

>   *FISHSELLER starts to leave. Stops.*

FISH SELLER   You're not making curry.

GRANNY   Yes, curry.

FISH SELLER   No. You must fry.

GRANNY   Why? No.

FISH SELLER   It's more work but it tastes much better.

GRANNY   Curry will do.

**FISH
SELLER**   Sorry. You must fry.

GRANNY   No.

**FISH
SELLER**   What?

GRANNY   I bought curry leaves.

**FISH
SELLER**   Use masala. Paprika.

GRANNY   I will make a curry and I will use tomato, onion, and
cumin.

**FISH
SELLER**   You will use coriander and chili powder and you will
fry – give me your word.

GRANNY   It's too much work.

**FISH
SELLER**   They're still my fish. I don't have to sell.

GRANNY   All right, fried, fried.

**FISH
SELLER**   Sign my sheet?

>   *FISHSELLER takes a form from his pocket.*

It's a petition. We want to start a union.

GRANNY   No.

**FISH
SELLER**   We need one. The coolies at the railway station – you
see how they work but they still make more than us.
Why? They have a union. People can change the way
they live.

GRANNY   I don't know how.

        FISHSELLER takes GRANNY's hand in his and signs the sheet for her.

Thank you.

        SERVANT GIRL enters.

FISH SELLER   Sign for a union?

        SERVANT GIRL signs the form.

SERVANT GIRL   I remember how you brushed my hair. What is it you remember? Something.

FISH SELLER   The ice is melting. My fish are starting to smell. *(hands her a fish)* Take. *(to GRANNY)* Fresh oil. And don't leave them long.

        FISHSELLER starts to ride away. Then stops.

I remember taking lessons at the post office. And finally being able to read the newspaper to you. But you fell asleep. This is what I remember. That first time.

Scene: India
—•—•—

        AUNTIE, TOMMY, and TINA watch the television. UNCLE enters.

UNCLE   What's this?

AUNTIE   Let them watch.

UNCLE   News. There will be no news in this house.

        UNCLE turns off the television.

        (to AUNTIE) What's wrong with you?

AUNTIE	Just once. What will it do?
UNCLE	Go to bed Tina.
AUNTIE	Go Tina.

> *TINA slides away. UNCLE turns on the television again.*

TOMMY	What's wrong?
AUNTIE	Each day in Kerala a beautiful woman is chosen by the state to read the news. The television producers drive through the streets looking for someone. Maybe she's waiting at a bus stop or selling mango pickle by the side of the road. They pick a woman and she calls her family and her family calls more people. That night everyone watches.
UNCLE	For 30 minutes her face is seen all over the state. What does she get paid? At the end of the broadcast she gets to keep her sari. You should understand the pain this causes. It is better not to know these things.

> *UNCLE turns off the television and covers it back up with a white cotton sheet to protect from dust. UNCLE leaves. TOMMY leaves.*

AUNTIE	Tina. Tina!

> *TINA returns.*

Today at the sari store – you should have been excited. You can be. Your marriage won't be like this one. Eventually you will be unhappy but not in the beginning. You will understand all that I'm saying when your marriage becomes like mine. Even now though. Despite my sadness, I think about leaving your father sometimes and my legs can still turn like yours.

Scene: Canada
—•—•—

*Night. TOMMY lies asleep in the cornfield.
GRANNY approaches and starts to make a rice
pattern around her sleeping grandson.*

GRANNY   Idiot! Pervert.

TOMMY   Granny! What are you doing here?

GRANNY   The things you're doing tonight. You're making me
ashamed.

TOMMY   Make me feel better.

GRANNY   You think you can just forget India?

> *Beat.*

Snow.

> *GRANNY holds out her hand and spins, catching
> snow.*

TOMMY   Granny. How old are you?

GRANNY   I don't know.

TOMMY   When's your birthday?

GRANNY   I don't know.

TOMMY   What's it say on your birth certificate?

GRANNY   I don't have one.

TOMMY   You have a license?

GRANNY   For a car? No! I've lived without these things all my
life.

TOMMY   Maybe you're a hundred.

GRANNY	Oh, more than that.
TOMMY	Really? No. Old people are supposed to tell the truth.

GRANNY opens her mouth to catch snow.

GRANNY	Like rain. But sweeter.
TOMMY	I want to stop thinking about Tina. Tell me how.
GRANNY	What do you think happened to her?
TOMMY	I don't know. She died.
GRANNY	She died! Why you say that?
TOMMY	She did. No?
GRANNY	She arranges shoes when people go into the Taj Mahal.
TOMMY	What? No. She's been missing six months. She's not still alive.
GRANNY	She lives in Vellore and eats rose water ice cream for breakfast. In the afternoon she goes to the cinema and watches Hindi movies from the balcony. A jasmine ponytail.
TOMMY	Stop it Granny. She's dead. Like Grandpa.
GRANNY	Grandpa was an old man. Tina is a young girl.
TOMMY	You should go.
GRANNY	*(mocking)* She was hit by a train then.

TOMMY throws snow.

TOMMY	You like how this feels?
GRANNY	*(mocking)* She was run over by a lorry.
TOMMY	It's snowing.

GRANNY   She's sliding. Wandering. Trying to find a home. She left you Tommy but she didn't die. She's alive somewhere. Happy even.

> *TOMMY throws snow.*

TOMMY   An avalanche.

GRANNY   Where is she?

> *TOMMY punches GRANNY, finally silencing her. She lies still.*

TOMMY   *(talks to the sky)* Tina. It's me again. I know I said I'd never talk to you anymore but I want you to do something. I think you're in heaven but I need to know for sure. Where are you? Show me.

> *TOMMY looks at GRANNY on his ground.*

You were supposed to help me.

> *TOMMY lies on the ground, resting his head on GRANNY's chest.*

Scene: India
—•—•—

> *The FISHSELLER perspires as he delivers baskets of fish. He encounters the SERVANT GIRL.*

SERVANT GIRL   You stink.

FISH SELLER   I'm hot.

SERVANT GIRL   Your hands are filthy.

FISH SELLER   I'm going to rub your skin.

SERVANT GIRL	Get away from me!
FISH SELLER	You used to lie on top of me. You forget that?
SERVANT GIRL	The way you'd lick my body and wouldn't stop – Che!
FISH SELLER	Your tongue.
SERVANT GIRL	Your tongue.
FISH SELLER	And my finger.
SERVANT GIRL	I remember.

Silence.

FISH SELLER	I have to work.

Scene: India
—•—•—

Front porch. TINA designs her pattern, wearing a scarf in her hair. TOMMY enters, hiding something in his hands.

TINA   You smell different.

TOMMY   I was running in the cinnamon field. I bought you a present.

TINA   What is it?

TOMMY blows the whistle then hands it to TINA.

TOMMY   Blow.

> *The girl blows. TOMMY takes the whistle back, blows,*
> *then hands it back to his cousin who blows again.*

Like kissing.

TINA   The women are inside frying fish. Then they will
make chicken curry. Then dahl and rice. 800 guests
are expected tomorrow. They will sit in the garden.
The children will run then hide in the folds of their
mother's sari. The men will smoke beadies, the
richer ones, Charminars. They will drink toddy and
Kingfisher. It will be sunny. The bride hasn't met her
husband yet. He has been told about her legs but she
knows he will still be disappointed when he sees her.
He will think her ugly. In time he will learn how to
move around her body but he will always touch her as
if she is a bird. He will keep her in the house. I am
Tina Chandy. This ends our broadcast.

> *TINA undoes the scarf in her hair, and covers her face*
> *as the television is covered by a tablecloth to protect it*
> *from dust.*

I want to show you my legs.

TOMMY   Are they bad?

TINA   Yes.

> *TINA raises her dress to reveal her damaged legs.*

TOMMY   I knew they were ugly but not this much.

TINA   Touch them. Try.

> *TOMMY forces himself to touch her legs.*

No one else will ever do that.

TOMMY   Your husband.

TINA   No.

TOMMY   Let's go somewhere special tonight.

TINA	You should go alone.
TOMMY	I don't want to.
TINA	I have to get ready for tomorrow. I need to take rest.
TOMMY	But it's the last time.
TINA	No. Where will you go?
TOMMY	I'm not telling you. It was someplace really nice.
TINA	You can tell me everything in the morning.
TOMMY	No. You'll always wonder where I went but you'll never know.

TOMMY exits.

Scene: India
—•—•—

Kitchen. The women prepare food. Lots of activity. UNCLE enters.

GRANNY	Leave.
UNCLE	Show me how you make what we eat.
GRANNY	You don't need to know this. I'll cook for you.
UNCLE	And when you're gone? *(to AUNTIE)* What are you making?
AUNTIE	Naan. Get flour. Get a bowl.

AUNTIE hands her bowl to UNCLE.

Touch with your hands. Mix with me.

AUNTIE takes his hand in hers.

Touch with your fingers. Keep it warm or it will spoil.

UNCLE and AUNTIE knead together.

Scene: India
—•—•—

*Evening. TINA sits on her bed under a mosquito net.
GRANNY, AUNTIE, and SERVANT GIRL enter.*

TINA   What is it mother?

*The women sit on the bed and put their hands under the
covers, touching TINA's body.*

GRANNY   Tomorrow night your husband will touch you here.

AUNTIE   Here.

GRANNY   Here.

AUNTIE   Here.

GRANNY   Here.

**SERVANT
GIRL**   For a brief moment it will feel wonderful.

UNCLE appears at the door.

UNCLE   Are you coming to bed?

AUNTIE   I was going to sleep beside Tina tonight.

UNCLE   Yes. It is your last night to be with her.

*UNCLE exits. AUNTIE kisses TINA then follows
after her husband to their bedroom.*

Scene: India
—•—•—

Night. TOMMY and TINA in the city. The NUT SELLER sits on a mat hawking cashews.

NUT SELLER   Sweet sweet. Sweet Nuts.

TOMMY   You want cashews?

TINA   No.

TOMMY   You want a Cadbury's?

TINA   No.

TOMMY   You're not saying anything.

NUT SELLER   Sweet sweet. Sweet Nuts.

TINA   I want to be quiet.

TOMMY   Why did you change your mind and come to the city if you're going to be like this? We've wandered all over, the places we always go, but you're not having fun. What happened Wife? You don't like me anymore?

NUT SELLER   Sweet sweet. Sweet Nuts.

TINA   Why did you show me all this? If I had never left the porch. If I had just stayed where I always was.

TOMMY   Let's go back.

TINA   You go first. I've never come home by myself. I want to see if I can. I should do something on my own, once in my life.

TOMMY   I'm not leaving you.

TINA	I'm leaving you. Tomorrow I get married. Go. Do the rice pattern for me.
TOMMY	You like your husband more than me?
	Silence.
TINA	Go home Tommy. Wait for your bride.
NUT SELLER	Sweet sweet. Sweet nuts.
TOMMY	You're going to get hurt.
TINA	Trust me.
TOMMY	I don't like you. You always get what you want.
	TOMMY exits. The NUT SELLER follows him.
NUT SELLER	Sweet-Sweet, Sweet nuts.

Scene: India
—•—•—

Early morning. TOMMY sits high in the tree. AUNTIE, GRANNY, and SERVANT GIRL rush onto the porch.

AUNTIE	Have you seen Tina?
GRANNY	She's not at the grave.
SERVANT GIRL	She's not inside.
AUNTIE	Climb the tree Tommy.
	TOMMY climbs higher.

Where is she? What do you see?

TOMMY	I don't know. What happened?

TOMMY collapses from the tree and lies still on the ground. AUNTIE runs into the house.

AUNTIE	Husband! Why did I sleep beside you?

Scene: Canada
—•—•—

Late at night. FATHER walks with a flashlight. He comes upon TOMMY shivering under a tree. He touches his son.

FATHER	Tommy! What are you doing?
TOMMY	You woke up.
FATHER	I'm so cold. Feel.

FATHER touches TOMMY's face with his hands. TOMMY touches his own face. Then his FATHER's.

TOMMY	There's no difference.
FATHER	I found you.

FATHER sits beside his son, under the tree. The following plays around them:

India. The front porch. Sound of a large celebration. GRANNY, AUNTIE, and SERVANT GIRL are dressed in saris. UNCLE enters.

GRANNY	Have you found Tina?
UNCLE	We've looked all over. The guests know something is wrong.
GRANNY	Where's the groom?
UNCLE	Crying in the taxi. His father punched me.

GRANNY   Where could she go?

UNCLE   A big wedding. A honeymoon. A good marriage and healthy baby. I want to feel these things, where is she? What should we do mother? The yard is full of people. All see the same thing: failure as a husband, now a failure as a father.

                 AUNTIE embraces her husband.

AUNTIE   She doesn't want to be married.

                 FISHSELLER enters with a banana leaf plate full of fish.

FISH SELLER Congratulations Auntie – the fish is excellent! I told you.

                 Noticing his ex-wife:

                 I remember our wedding.

SERVANT GIRL Long ago, you spread your fish smell all over me, onto my body, into my hair. I am clean now. And beautiful. But I'm always sad.

FISH SELLER You are still just the Servant Girl and I am still just a Fish Seller. We are not like them. But you think that you are.

SERVANT GIRL Go. Bring me some fish. I will eat from your fingers. Then wipe your hands on my shoulders.

FISH SELLER I want to sail toward you. From a distance, you look like the place you once were. But you are not that place anymore.

UNCLE   I have lost my daughter.

AUNTIE   You still have your wife.

TOMMY   What happened to my mother? Where is she?

FATHER   She's in heaven. You know that.

TOMMY   And Tina?

FATHER   I don't know. Also in heaven.

TOMMY   What if she's still alive?

FATHER   Who can say?

TOMMY   Is she sliding around? Wandering? Tell me. Where is she?

FATHER   I don't know. Is it better to think that they're dead? Try.

TOMMY   I want to forget. Tina. India. Everything.

FATHER   What you want me to do? You want me to say all the answers will come? I hope so but I don't know. Ache is heavy. Makes the body go slow. But maybe someday the pain floats away. Okay?

TOMMY   I want to change who I am but no one wants me. Not even a father whose son disappeared.

FATHER   Talk when we get home. It's cold.

   FATHER starts to walk toward home but TOMMY remains seated.

TOMMY   I'm not Canadian.

FATHER   I told you.

TOMMY   I'm still not Indian.

FATHER   What are you then?

   Silence.

TOMMY   Big people are supposed to help. I'm too little.

FATHER   I'm like you. You go from point A to point B. Then
              back to A. Then back to B. In between. Living
              nowhere. Not Canadian but not Indian.

TOMMY   All of us are the same.

FATHER   The father and the son.

TOMMY   Tina and Mom.

FATHER   No. They're gone. In heaven. Or India. But I'm here.
              Beside you. In Canada. Now. Just the two of us.

**SERVANT
GIRL**   Tina never comes home. There is no wedding. The
              guests eat then leave.

UNCLE   Uncle starts to watch the news, each night hoping to
              see his daughter.

              *UNCLE turns on the television, faint light as the set
              warms up.*

GRANNY   Granny dies.

              GRANNY exits.

UNCLE   Uncle and Auntie stay together many years until one
              day he gets kicked in the stomach by a cow.

AUNTIE   She runs to get the doctor but it is too late.

              UNCLE and AUNTIE exit.

**SERVANT
GIRL**   The Servant Girl and the Fish Seller never get back
              together. Sometimes she closes her eyes and he
              brushes her hair again but then the communists
              come to power and the Fish Seller moves to the port.

**FISH
SELLER** He waits for the government to give him a boat. Years later, he finally buys his own. In an old boat, the old man sets sail for Sri Lanka but he never gets there.

FISHSELLER exits.

**SERVANT
GIRL** The Servant Girl doesn't know this. The rest of her life she keeps waiting for the Fish Seller to return to her. She thinks of him praying for Kingfish, throwing the mermaids back into the sea.

SERVANT GIRL exits.

FATHER No more talking to ghosts.

TOMMY You can't stop.

FATHER I will. I promise. *(shouts to the sky)* Goodbye Wife.

FATHER moves into the dark.

Husband is gone but Father is still there. Not a good one okay, but who else you get? I'll be the house. Walk on the driveway. Knock on the door. Come Tommy. Let's go home.

TOMMY starts to spin in circles.

What are you doing?

TOMMY *(shouts to the sky)* Goodbye Wife.

FATHER steps from the dark and starts spinning. TOMMY collapses.

FATHER *(shouts to the sky)* Good-bye Wife.

FATHER collapses. TOMMY stands and starts spinning again. He collapses at a distance from his FATHER.

Come close Tommy. Not a straight line. Do zigzag. We're the same. Boys without girls.

Both are dizzy. They stand then collapse then stand again, staggering, struggling toward each other.

The world is spinning. Flipping. Can you see me? Try.

TOMMY   I see you.

Blackout.

The end.

Sunil Kuruvilla has developed his plays at such theatres as New York Theatre Workshop, Williamstown Theatre Festival, and Portland Centre Stage. He has received commissions from the Joseph Papp Public Theatre, The Wilma Theater, and South Coast Repertory. The Canada Council for the Arts and the Ontario Arts Council have generously and steadily supported his work. Kuruvilla has also written screenplays for CTV and "Showtime." He has a Master's degree in creative writing from the University of Windsor and a Master's degree in playwriting from the Yale School of Drama. His favourite food is corn-on-the-cob, buttered, lightly salted.